Chasing a Chicken & Catching a Cow

A Reflective Account

Onyekachi Ezulike

Prologue

Chasing a chicken and catching a cow is a reflective account of the author's sojourn from a remote village in Nigeria to Coventry University, UK, where he won a highly coveted and contested internship position with a conglomerate, and went on to graduate with a Masters Degree with Distinction in International Business. This reflective writing is based on conducting a real life marketing research for Thomson Overseas Property Investment, UK, aimed at creating a blueprint and giving holiday villas in Peyia, Cyprus the competitive edge they needed to compete all year round in the global holiday rental market.

Beyond the challenges of a rigorous research, this reflective account shows the intricacies and unique perspectives of a village boy who made it to boardrooms in the U.K. private sector and performed at the highest levels; the cultural & class differences and challenges even in the most professional environments. It's a short and palatable read for everyone.

Chapter 1

"Don't lower your expectations to meet your performance. Raise your level of performance to meet your expectations"

It was a journey in every sense of the word, which started with the enthusiasm of a tourist going abroad on holiday. I had no idea of the internship program prior to my being admitted to Coventry University for a Masters Degree in International Business, but then once I got the wind of it, I started to get more information about it, regarding the array of opportunities it offered.

Among all the reasonable hypothesised benefits of getting selected for internship, what appealed to me the most, which I eagerly looked forward to, were application of classroom knowledge, gaining confidence and valuable work experience, relatively easier access to the job market without having to go through the pushing and shoving and volatility, and the only opportunity for a 'trial and error.' Also, it would be the first time I would be working on a real life project and being relied on to yield results. So, it was a huge responsibility in my opinion.

"Don't lower your expectations to meet your performance. Raise your level of performance to meet your expectations. Expect the best of yourself, and then do what is necessary to make it a reality." (ThinkExist 2011)

This quote by Ralph Marston best put my mindset before the Masters internship in perspective. I already knew how competitive it was going to be, but I was very expectant at the same time. Having rated myself objectively, I expected to breeze through CV submission. In fact, I thought my challenges would commence from the presentation and interview stage, so most of the homework I did was based on how to give a good presentation and interview.

Coventry University Business School intentionally designed the process to be tough and highly competitive, to ensure that only the best candidates are presented to partner firms. Preceding the presentation and interview stage was the CV submission stage, however, to get picked one must submit a winning CV and must have also attended all the compulsory leadership lectures from CEOs of Fortune 500 companies, and scored above 60% in all the completed modules thus far, and I did.

However, after submitting my CV, I got a message from the internship team saying that my CV made the cut but I was disqualified on the grounds that I didn't attend all the leadership lectures. I was convinced that there must have been a mix-up somewhere, so I got in touch with them and the issue was resolved accordingly. I went through the presentation and interview very smoothly, as I was constantly in contact with Kevin Coyne of the Employability and Placements unit, who was very helpful. Bottom line, I was selected! Thus the chase began.

All the selected internship students had a meeting with Jody Holland, the Head of Department, where she put us through the module and what was expected of us. More importantly however, she told us categorically that at that stage we were in direct competition with each other to secure a place for internship, because we will all be applying to the same partner companies. We were meant to go through the availability projects/placements on the portal and apply to three companies/projects. I was quite lucky because out of my first three picks, two companies invited me for interview.

The first company needed to form a strategic marketing group (group internship), which I picked because I wanted to have a firsthand experience of working in a group with real life project and the challenges and dynamics of being in a team and chasing a deadline.

Unfortunately, I missed the interview because of a clash with a presentation I had for another Business Law module. This made the build-up to the second interview very intense, because I approached it with the mindset of having all my eggs in one basket. I already heard of students who couldn't secure a place early and the resultant effects, and I didn't want to be in the same situation.

Chapter 2

"To whom much is given…"

Coming into the internship, my strategy was to play it safe; therefore I was very tactical when picking my first three companies/projects. I wanted something that would pose a calculated challenge, expose me to all the experiences and leave me more informed, skilled and equipped than I was when I started. I was being ambitious without being unrealistic. However, one glance told me that almost every project is directly or indirectly connected to marketing and business development.

Having had no prior background whatsoever in marketing, it was a different kind of challenge altogether but I embraced it. I strategically picked a project that entailed conducting a research and producing a Marketing Plan for 197 student rental houses owned by Thomson Overseas Property Investment, UK, because I felt it was something I would excel in, so I thought 'job half done'.

While preparing for the interview, I did my homework and put a document together detailing my ideas on how to market the student housing units and budget. When the day came, I dressed the part and proceeded to the interview. When I met Warren Dunn, Thomson OPI's Director who would go on to be my mentor on the project, he immediately told me not to think of this as a typical interview. "Let's just sit and throw ideas around," he said to me. This relaxed me a great deal.

I handed him the document I had prepared and he seemed surprised, flipped through it and nodded his head several times before extracting my CV from a pile on his table. After throwing some ideas around about the student housing units and other projects he had on the table, he then told me what he had in mind for me. According to him, two things made him select me for interview, first, I studied BSc Economics like he did, but unlike him I made a first class. He laughed so I followed suit. Secondly, I studied in Cyprus, so he had a perfect project for me, which was based in Cyprus, because he thinks I am best suited for it and can bring a unique perspective to the project. It may also require traveling to Cyprus.

However, he said to avoid giving me something I didn't want to do, I should go home, think about it and then get back to him in 24 hours with my top three choices out of all the projects we had discussed earlier. He then applauded me for the document I put together, saying I should definitely do that in future job interviews because it shows preparedness, self-starting and attention to details.

Having tactically avoided this particular project at first, because I felt it would be gruelling, I gave it a second thought and made it my second choice. I was eventually given the Cyprus project, and then it dawned on me the responsibility I had just been given. I was nervous, and surprised but grateful. For the first time in my career I had a project all to myself, with a £60,000 budget, to make or break. This meant that someone trusted in my ability to be versatile even when I hardly knew that about myself, which made me play safe at first.

It literally put fire in my belly and I immediately braced up to my responsibilities, including everything that came with it like decision-making, time management, rigour and project management.

This conforms to the incentive theory of motivation; the incentive here being to earn the trust and responsibility that has been given to me (Cherry 2011). It also follows Maslow's humanistic theory of motivation, citing that motivation is influenced by need and human beings follow a particular hierarchy of needs according to pre-potency; meaning that there is an emergence of a new need following the satisfaction of the proponent need (Maslow 1987). The need for people to recognise my personal worth, applaud or trust me (Esteem Needs) preceded the need for me to establish myself in a chosen career via my work (Self-actualising needs). Therefore, once I was trusted with that responsibility, it motivated and guided me through self-actualisation.

My versatile, cognitive and charismatic natures were unlocked. This particular project entailed speaking to a lot of professionals and CEOs on the phone and sending dozens of emails, and so I leant to make a good first impression, which is vital for a manager and a leader.

I developed the ability to influence others while constantly seeking to expand my horizon, in order to unlock more hidden abilities. Consequently, 'hesitation' and 'playing-safe' metamorphosed to calculated risk-taking.

I also leant to not limit myself or ideas; the more I accomplished with my research the more motivated I became and the more ideas I got and the harder I worked except it didn't feel like it, and it seemed I had endless possibilities.

I was hungry for application of ideas and results. It also taught me a lesson about believing in other people, when there is something to believe in, because the downside of being a perfectionist is not trusting other people to do the same job and as well or even better.

Chapter 3

"Reality check..."

My most important revelation came on the 5th of September 2011. My mentor, Warren Dunn, after putting me through my project and what was expected of me, gave me a long list of people I may need to contact, to get started with gathering the information and data I needed. He told me he would introduce me to the people I pick from the list.

One of these people that I selected happens to be a Group Account Manager, and I picked him out because at the time his company recently started providing redemption services for property owners in Cyprus who were having all sorts or problems with their properties, ranging from falling behind on mortgage payments to lack of buyers. I sent him an email, introducing myself sequel to Warren's introductory email. I then went straight to the point to avoid giving him too much to read or wasting his time, and then thanked him accordingly.

I used the same template to write the other four people and I got very helpful replies from them; some of them wanting to meet with me in person for further explanation and discussion on how my project could benefit their organisations.

But then I got this reply from Mr. T blatantly telling me that my email was very rude because according to him, I "intentionally avoided the use of words and phrases like 'please', 'I am sure you are a very busy person but…,' therefore, I think you need to revise this email again."

He made a copy to my mentor as well, so I was perplexed and upset by his reply because he totally caught me off guard. I needed to react immediately and so my first instinct bothering on 'two wrongs cannot make a right' was to apologise to him for whatever he perceived to be rude. Doing so disarmed him and deescalated the situation.

This happenstance is in line with Coser's theory of conflict and resolution. He thinks that conflict is instinctual for humans, so can be found everywhere in the society, triggered by the most unbelievable things, mainly to do with power, status and class.

Coser also thinks that this is a normal and functional part of human existence and so to be aware and somewhat expectant makes it easier to deal with (Coser 2006).

This also conforms to Riessman's Helper theory, which depicts that an unequal relationship exist between the 'helper' and 'helpee', which could lead to self-efficacy, hence mutual benefit on the part of the helper, but more often than not leads to marginalisation of the helpee (Gartner and Riessman 1977). Objectively and logically speaking, I was not at fault, because one out of five people represents 80% success rate on my part.

From his consequent replies I deduced that Mr T felt I was given an unusual easy access to him. Thankfully, Warren backed me up and in an email to him used the word 'bully' a few times and there were apologies in the end.

However, that incident taught me a whole lot, gave me a rude reality check, increased my understanding, improved my self-knowledge and altered my sense of perception and expectation both in the work place and life in general.

This would go on to be of invaluable help to me as a leader. I have learnt to approach different people in identical situations differently, what is good for the goose may not be good for the gander, however, this fact is often overlooked because textbook knowledge entails that operational and managerial efficiency/effectiveness cannot be achieved appealing to everyone individually.

It also helped me to work for and expect the best, but give room for unexpected results or outcome, besides nothing is guaranteed. It gave me the mental ability and psychological robustness to deal with issues and matters arising, no matter how unexpected; the mental readiness is the difference between success and failure or blatant disaster in conflict situations.

My perfectionist persona thenceforth ended
where the persona of other people began. The
episode also taught me to be more
accommodating, to give room for imperfections
and irregularities, so as to handle them better
when they arise, especially when dealing with
other people.

Chapter 4

"Information vs common sense"

Especially in the beginning of my internship, information became very challenging, including information overload, conflicting information and lack of pure positivism. This was fuelled by the fact that there were lots of false publications going on about Cyprus and the Cyprus situation, everybody had a different version of the same situation, and it was chaos.

It was Ruth Anshen who said, "Information is not synonymous with knowledge. Information is only data..." That couldn't be truer, because conflicting first hand information constantly misled me, especially coming from my mentor. My first breakthrough was identifying that this was one of my greatest problems with the research, and then I discovered the essence of evaluation and the power of the evaluator (me).

This happened because I automatically took my mentor's side in the beginning of the research, which made me biased and consequently compounded my problems with information. But once I realised this and became neutral, every other thing fell into place and I was able to run a credible research by sharpening my contingent decision-making.

Evaluation is a powerful and strict discipline; the ability to assimilate, distinguish and still stay neutral, which is 'common sense' in a lay man's term, but contrary to popular belief, common sense is not that common.

This conforms to Will Shadish's radical Evaluation theory, citing that it is "who we are", which aids thoughtful judgment and no one needs overt training in evaluation, which brings diversity of talents, views and knowledge set to the field. Meaning that the position of the evaluator is the difference between a credible research and a failed one, a biased position yields a biased result (Mark 2011).

I used to be an advocate of pure positivism, which entails observations independently leading to knowledge and explanation, exclusive of interpretation. However, having had this experience made me value strict evaluation and rationality more; owing to the fact that overload of information lessens wisdom if not properly managed. Besides, its very easy to be biased without knowing it. I consequently learnt that a successful leader does not make decisions based on popular opinion or belief.

Don't Forget the Chicken & the Cow!

I started out pretty focused, knowing exactly what I wanted and how to gain all the advantages that the internship program had to offer, but in my focus were my limitations, needless to say limitations I built up myself.

However, ensuing events exposed me to the fact that internship is a period to go wild with ideas and imaginations, and the only chance I had to apply them to see the outcome without career threatening consequences. Innovation fuels development, both personal and corporate, but this is limited in the volatile corporate world because people are often encouraged to be versatile, but are left alone to suffer if the outcome is negative.

I passed through the system and let the system pass through me, making it a wholesome experience, which has influenced my life in general and would send me fort to my future career well grounded, ready and confident.

It was definitely an experience I would wish for every student to have, because now I simply couldn't wait to see what the future held for me. The entirety of my experience during the internship surpassed my expectations; hence it was tantamount to chasing a chicken, and catching a cow, the African metaphor for going after a price but ending up with a much bigger price. That cow was large enough to go round, in every company or corporate community I found myself in the nearest future, even as I worked hard to catch more cows.

Reference

Cherry, K. (2011) Theories of Motivation [online] available from <http://psychology.about.com/od/ psychologytopics/tp/theories-of-motivation.htm> [24 December 2011]

Coser, L. (1956) The Functions of Social Conflict. New York: Free Press

Gartner, A. and Riessman, F. (1977) Self-Help in the Human Services. California: Jossey-Bass Publishers

Mark, M. (2011) Evaluation Theory or What Are Evaluation Methods for? [Online] available from < http://www.hfrp.org/evaluation/the-evaluation-exchange/issue-archive/evaluation-methodology/ evaluation-theory-or-what-are-evaluation-methods-for> [25 December 2011]

Maslow, A. (1987) Motivation and Personality. 3rd edn. New York: Addison-Wesley

ThinkExist (2011) Quotation [online] available from <http://thinkexist.com/quotation/don-t_lower_your_expectations_to_meet_your/14490.html> [18 October 2011]

About the Author

Onyekachi George Ezulike (Chelsma) is a serial entrepreneur, the Founder & CEO of **Ezu-like Group (www.ezu-likegroup.com)**, a group of companies based in Nigeria with interests in Construction & Real Estates with **Ezu-like Construction Limited**; Agriculture with **Samsara AGRO Limited**; Petroleum marketing with **Chelsma Oil Limited**; Haulage with **Ezu-like Transport Limited**; E-Commerce with **Soroban Technologies Limited**; Water Bottling with **George Ezu-like Investment Limited**, owners of Chelsma Water & Spruce Water; and Renewable Energy and Recycling with **Green Republic Limited** (www.GreenRepublic.com.ng).

Before devoting his work full-time to Ezu-like Group, Onyekachi worked as Head of Business Development (Europe) at Planet Matters (Alderney) Limited UK, VTP Global LLP and VZW Global LLP, a UK based experiential branding and armchair-investment organisation, whose clients include Bank of England, IBM, Gap, Samsung, Time Warner, Kalashnikov, Tivo, and Coventry Universities. He was retained at Thomson Overseas Properties, UK as a Marketing Manager following his internship.

Onyekachi is a First Class graduate of Economics, from Eastern Mediterranean University, Cyprus. He also bagged a Masters Degree with Distinction in International Business, from Coventry University UK, and a Doctor of Business Administration.

www.ingramcontent.com/pod-product-compliance
Lightning Source LLC
Chambersburg PA
CBHW060931130726
48001CB00006B/2524